WORSHIP TOGETHER®
favorites
12 of today's most popular worship songs

for Kids

ISBN-13: 978-1-4234-2541-0
ISBN-10: 1-4234-2541-3

HAL•LEONARD®
CORPORATION

7777 W. BLUEMOUND RD. P.O. BOX 13819 MILWAUKEE, WI 53213

Visit Hal Leonard Online at
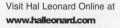
www.halleonard.com

ENOUGH

Words and Music by CHRIS TOMLIN
and LOUIE GIGLIO

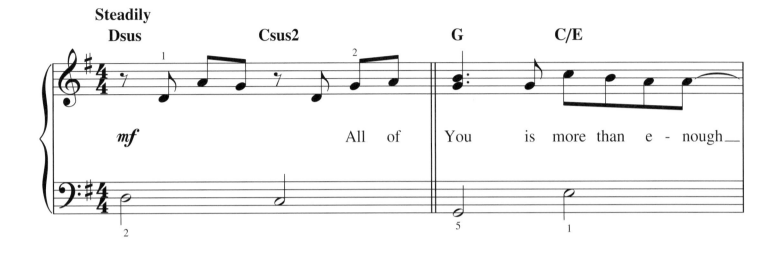

me with Your love,____ and all I have in

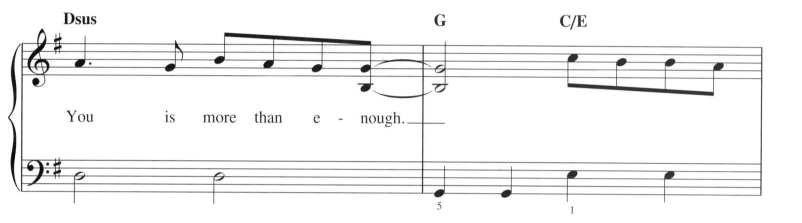

You is more than e - nough.____

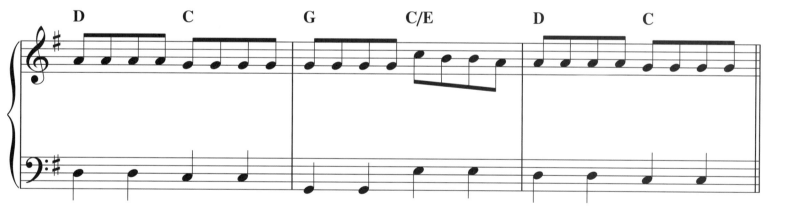

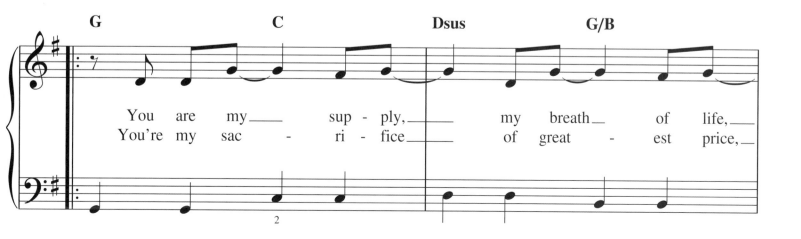

You are my____ sup - ply,____ my breath____ of life,____

You're my sac - ri - fice____ of great - est price,____

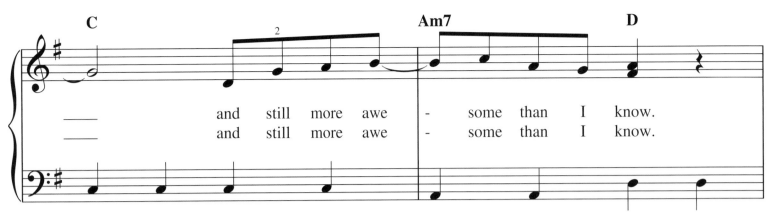

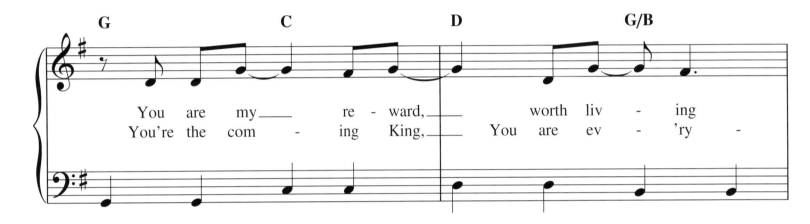

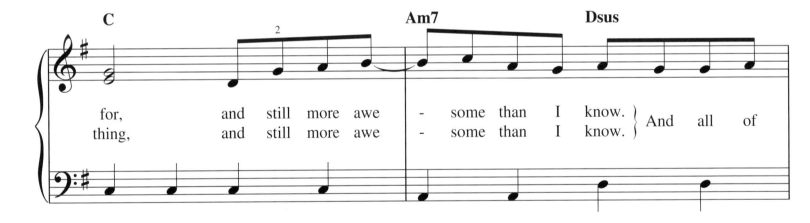

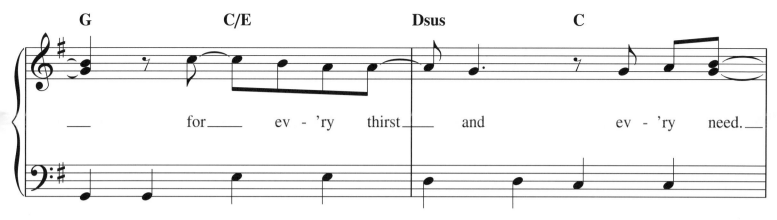

for__ ev - 'ry thirst__ and ev - 'ry need.__

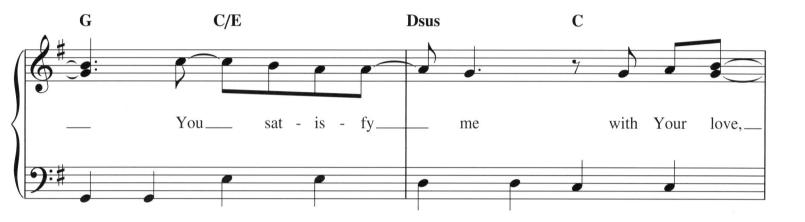

You__ sat - is - fy__ me with Your love,__

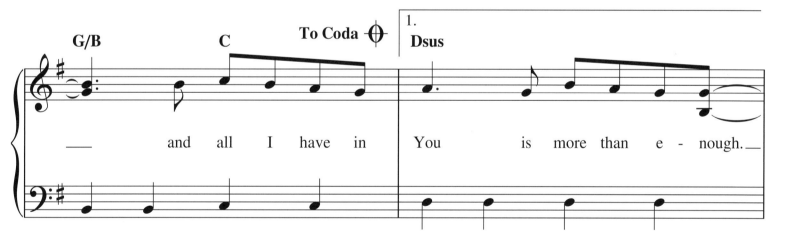

To Coda

1.

__ and all I have in You is more than e - nough.__

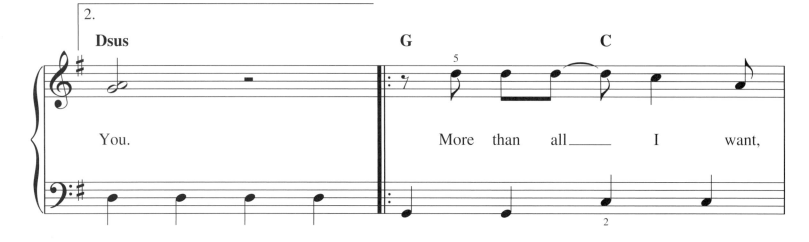

You.

More than all⎯ I want,

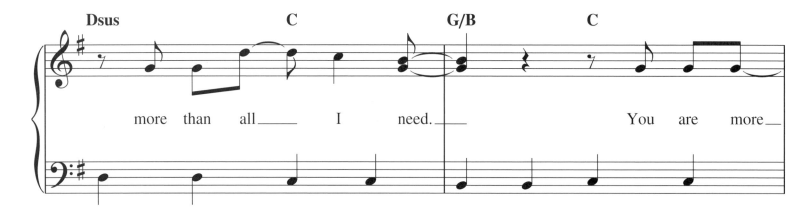

more than all⎯ I need.⎯ You are more⎯

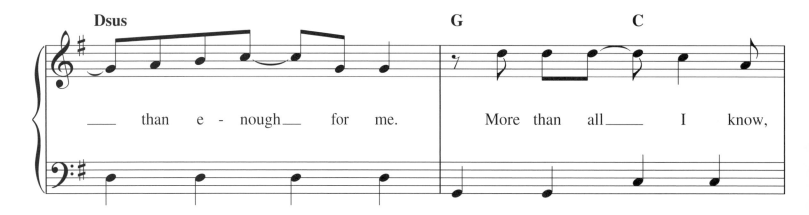

⎯ than e - nough⎯ for me. More than all⎯ I know,

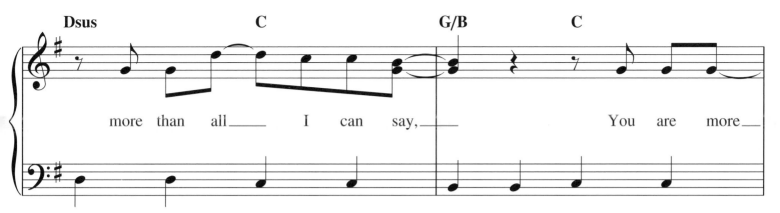

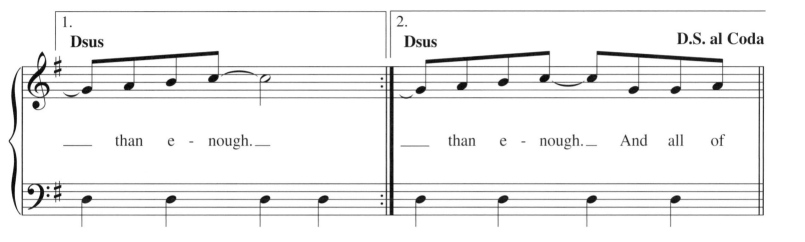

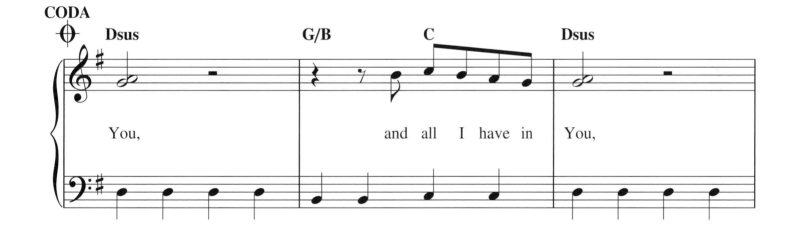

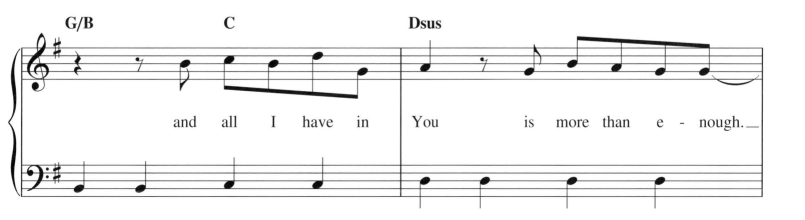

All of

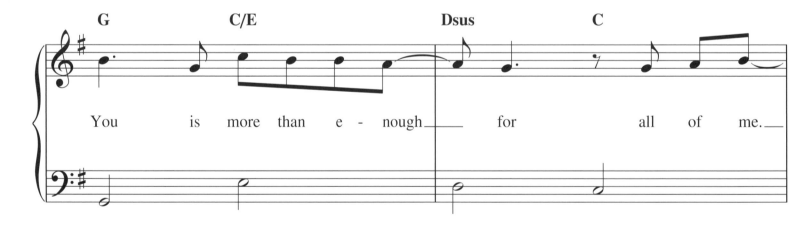

You is more than e - nough for all of me.

HOW GREAT IS OUR GOD

Words and Music by CHRIS TOMLIN,
JESSE REEVES and ED CASH

With praise

The

splen - dor of _____ a King, _____
age to age _____ He King stands, _____ and

clothed in maj - es - ty. _____ Let all the earth re -
time is in _____ His hands. _____ Be - gin - ning and the

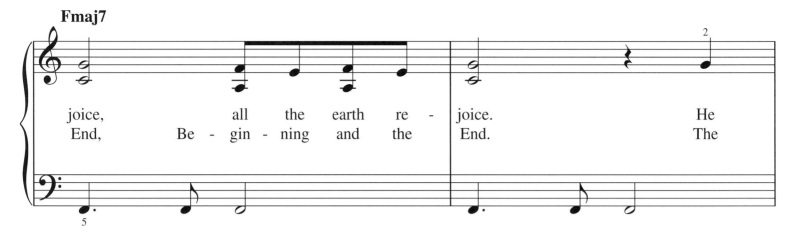

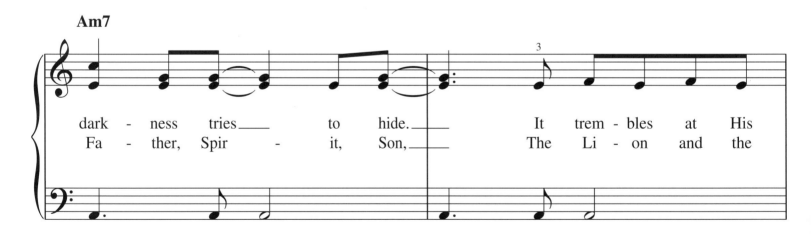

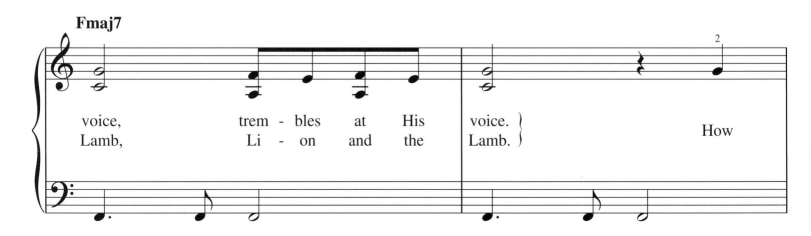

great   is our   God!   Sing   with   me: How

great   is our   God!   And   all   will   see   how

great,   how   great   is our   God!

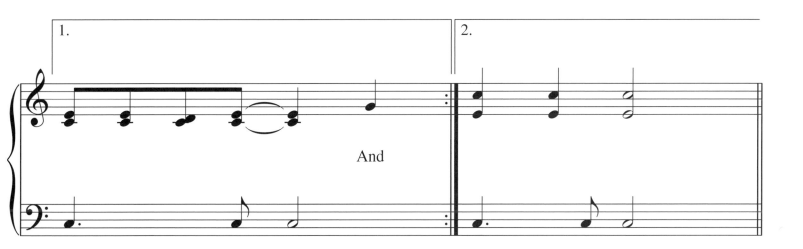

And

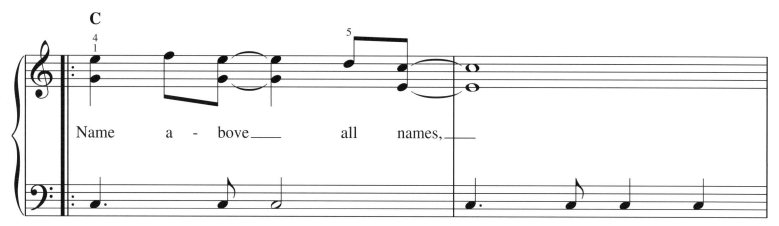

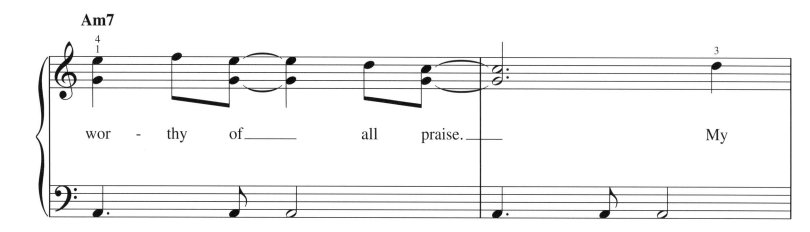

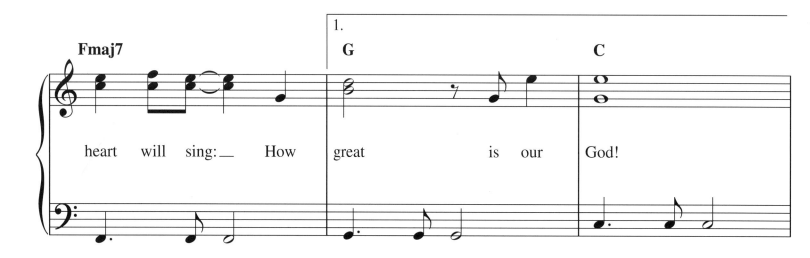

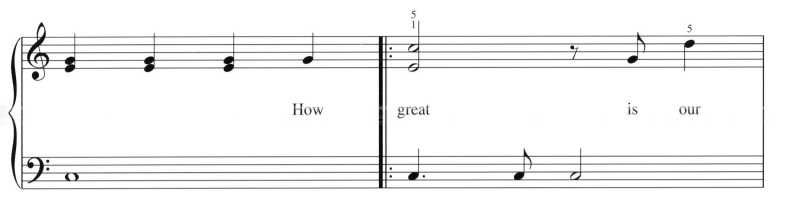

How great   is our

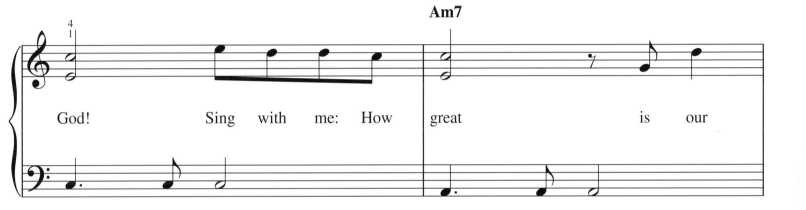

God!   Sing with me: How great   is our

Am7

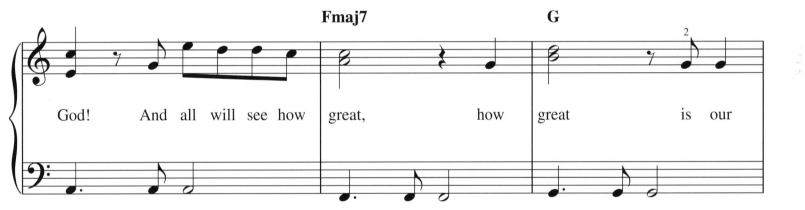

God!   And all will see how great,   how great   is our

Fmaj7   **G**

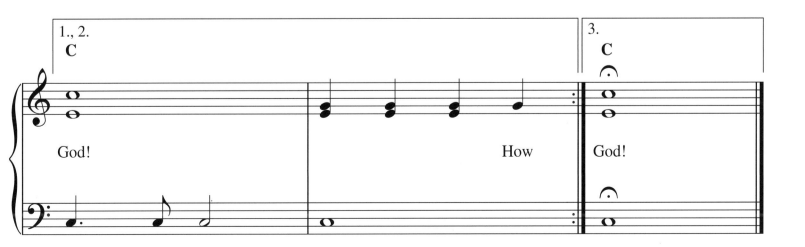

God!   How   God!

1., 2. **C**   3. **C**

EVERLASTING GOD

Words and Music by BRENTON BROWN
and KEN RILEY

Moderate Rock

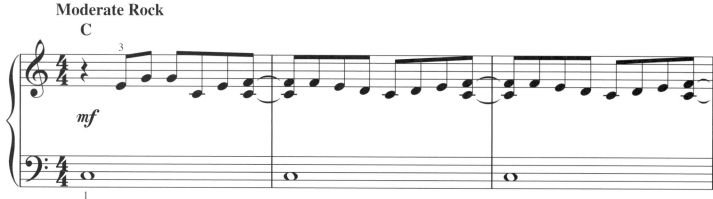

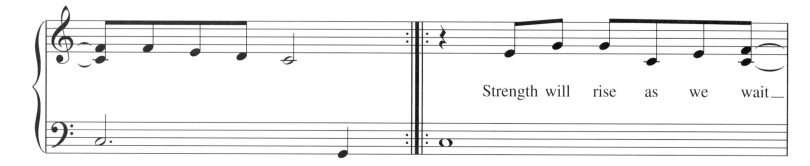

Strength will rise as we wait

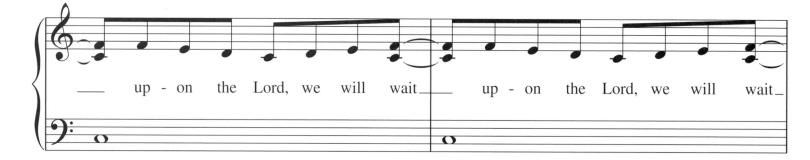

up - on the Lord, we will wait up - on the Lord, we will wait

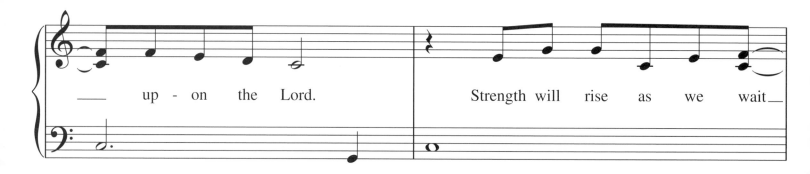

up - on the Lord. Strength will rise as we wait

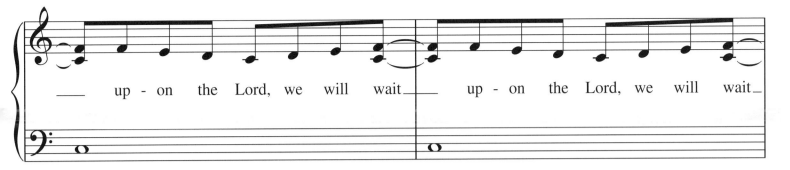

up - on the Lord, we will wait ___ up - on the Lord, we will wait ___

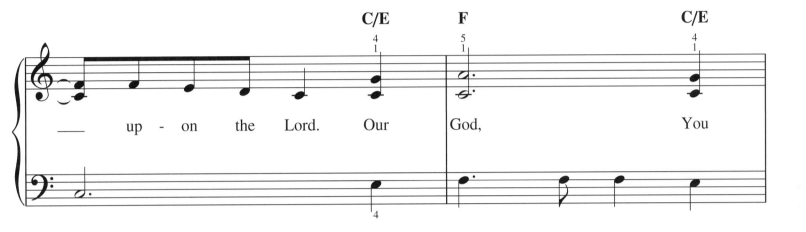

___ up - on the Lord. Our God, You

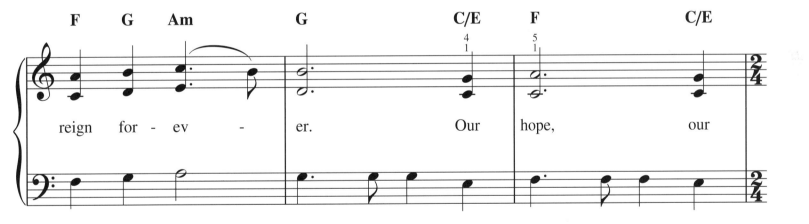

reign for - ev - er. Our hope, our

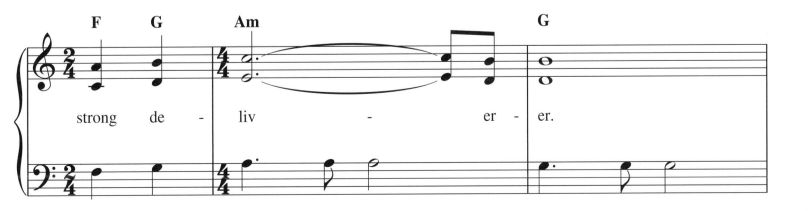

strong de - liv - er - er.

16

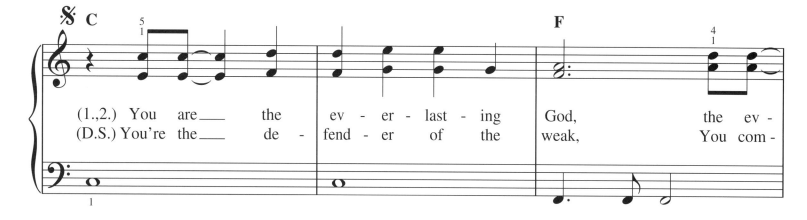

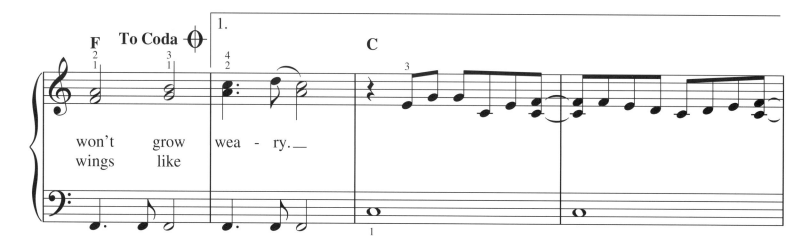

ea - gles.

Our

God, You reign for - ev - er. Our

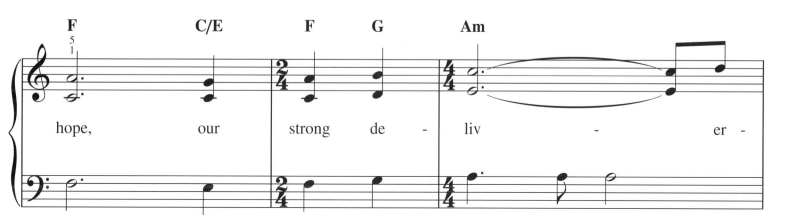

hope, our strong de - liv - er -

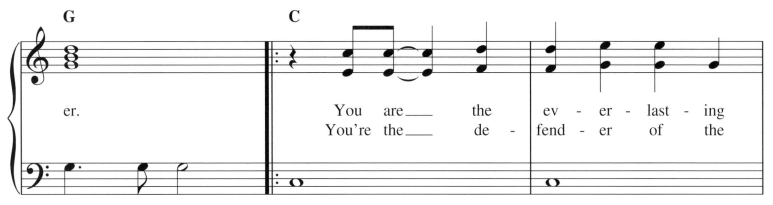

er.

You are___ the ev - er - last - ing
You're the___ de - fend - er of the

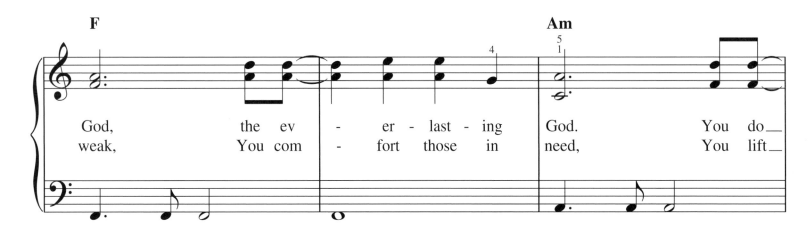

God, the ev - er - last - ing God. You do___
weak, You com - fort those in need, You lift___

___ not faint, You___ won't grow wea - ry.
___ us up on___ wings like

1.

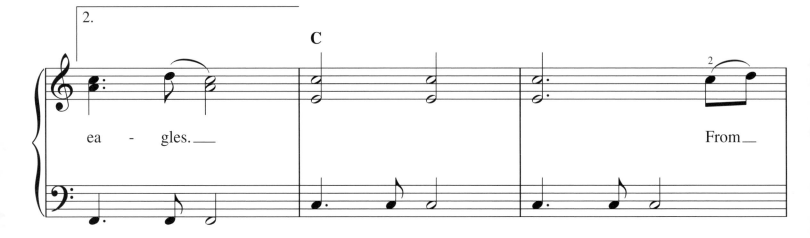

2.

ea - gles.___

From___

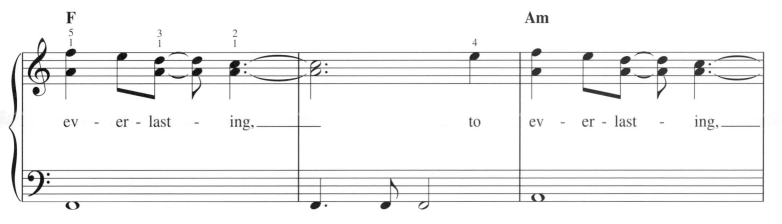

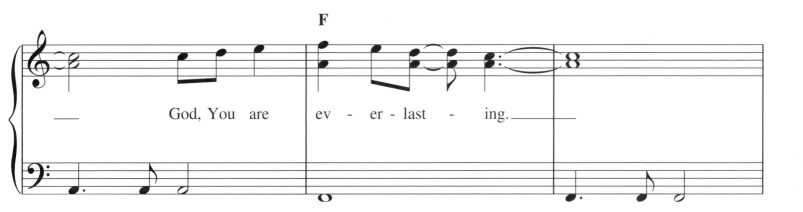

FOREVER

Words and Music by
CHRIS TOMLIN

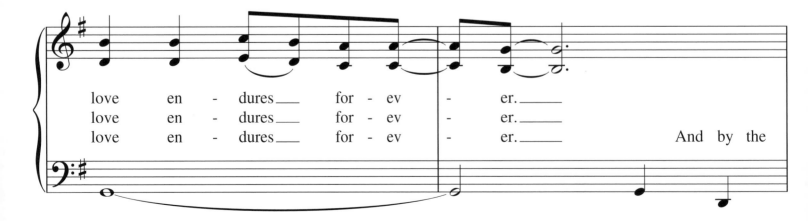

For He is good,___ He is a - bove all things.___ His
For the life___ that's been re - born,___ His
grace of God___ we will car - ry on.___ His

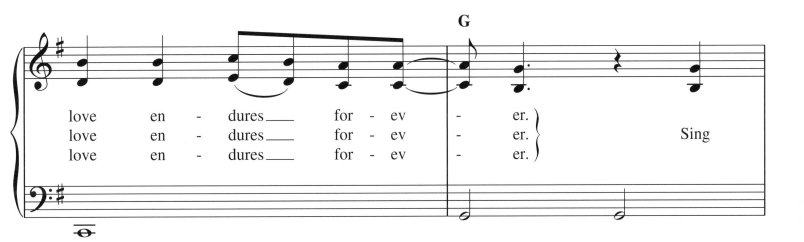

love en - dures___ for - ev - er.)
love en - dures___ for - ev - er.)
love en - dures___ for - ev - er.)   Sing

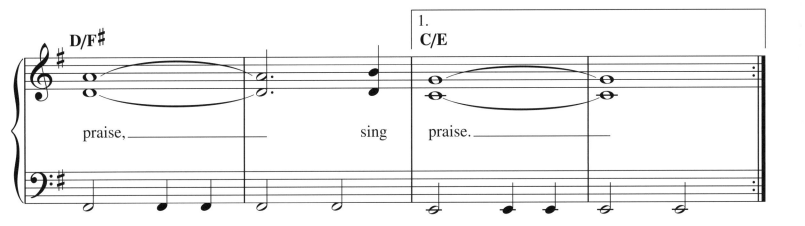

praise,___ ___ sing praise.___

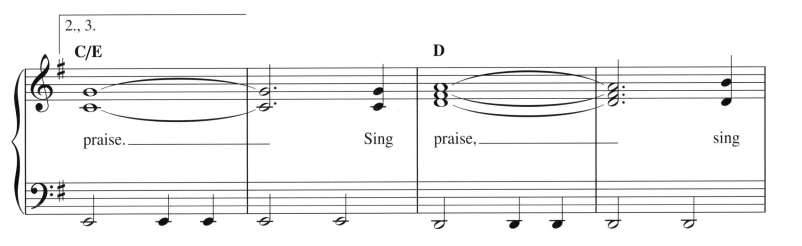

praise.___ ___ Sing praise,___ sing

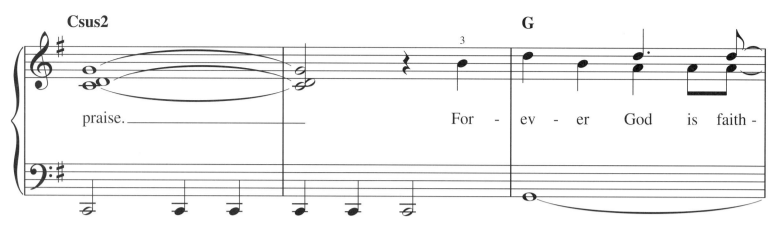

praise._____ For - ev - er God is faith-

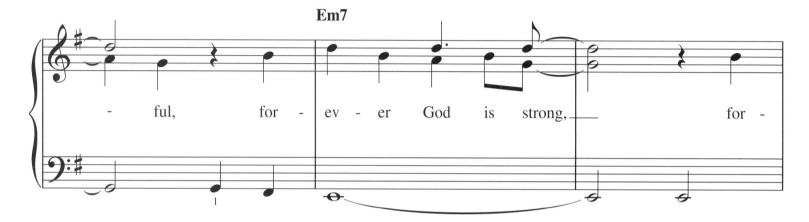

- ful, for - ev - er God is strong,_____ for -

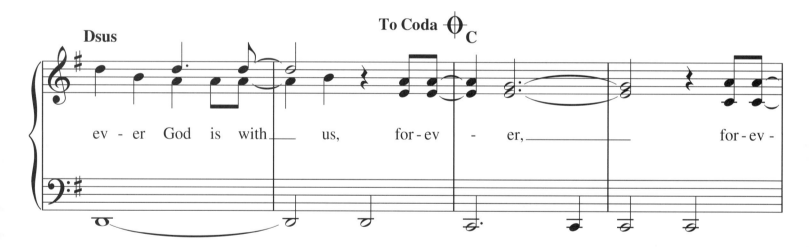

ev - er God is with___ us, for-ev - er,_____ for - ev -

- er._____

CODA

-er and ev - er and ev - er. For - ev - er God is faith-

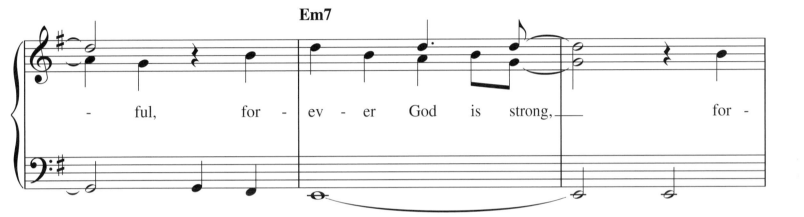

-ful, for - ev - er God is strong,_____ for -

ev - er God is with____ us, for - ev - er, for - ev-

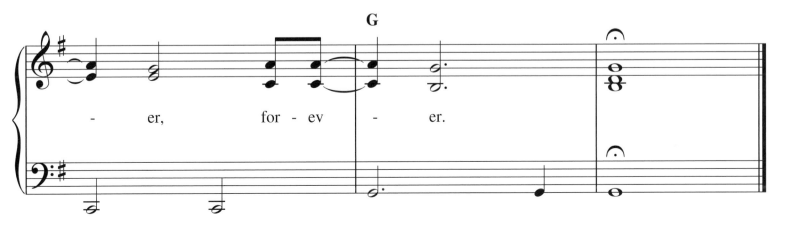

-er, for - ev - er.

FROM THE INSIDE OUT

Words and Music by
JOEL HOUSTON

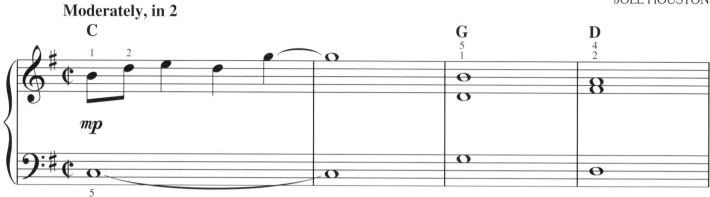

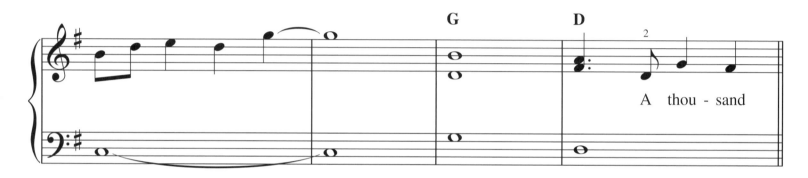

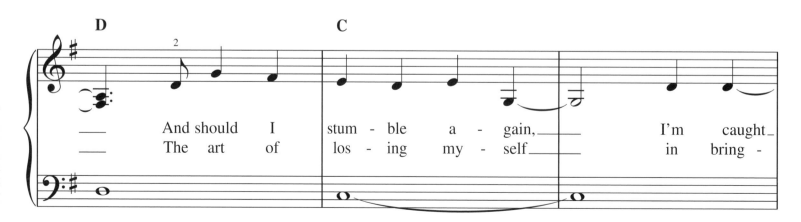

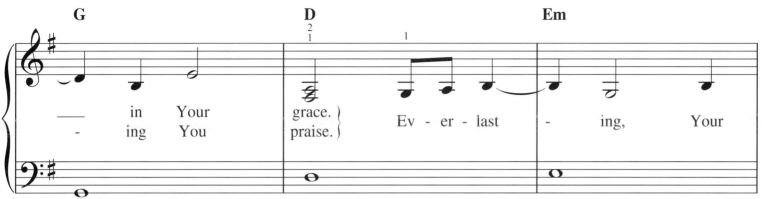

in Your
- ing You
grace.
praise.
Ev - er - last - ing, Your

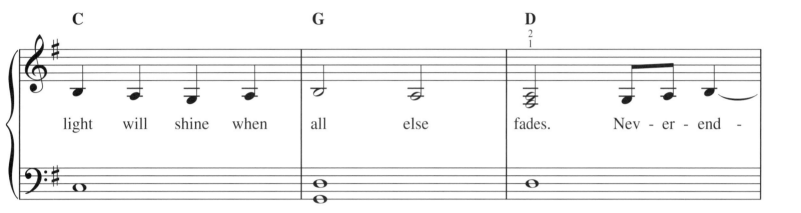

light will shine when all else fades. Nev - er - end -

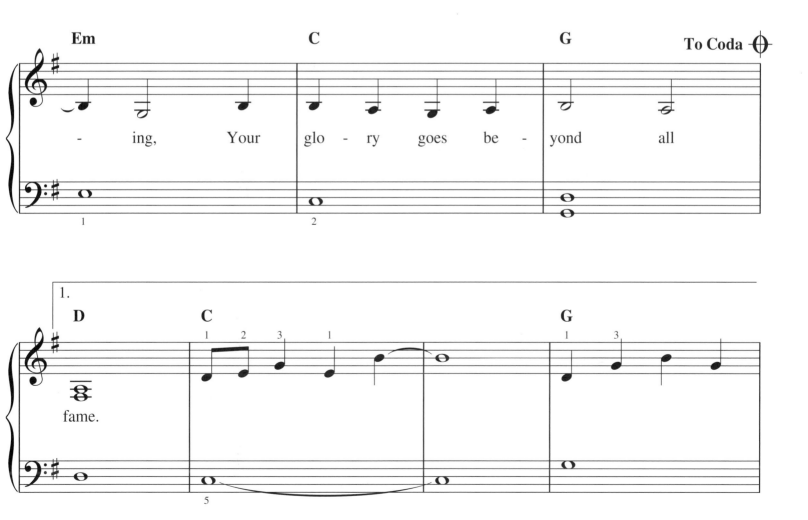

To Coda

- ing, Your glo - ry goes be - yond all

1.

fame.

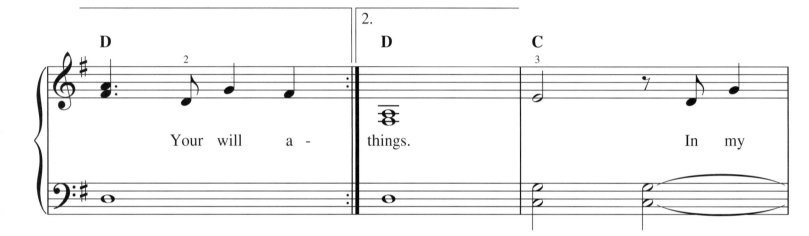

Your will a - things. In my

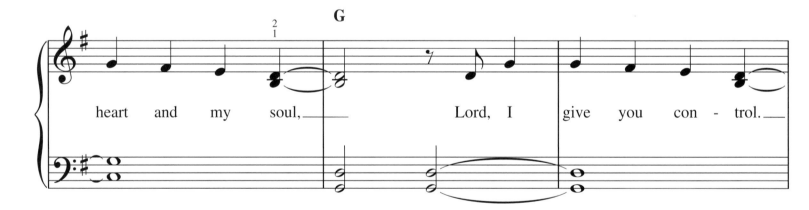

heart and my soul,___ Lord, I give you con - trol.___

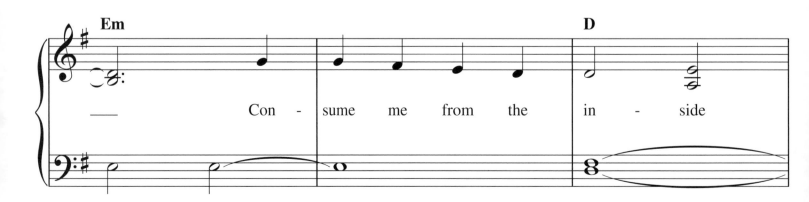

___ Con - sume me from the in - side

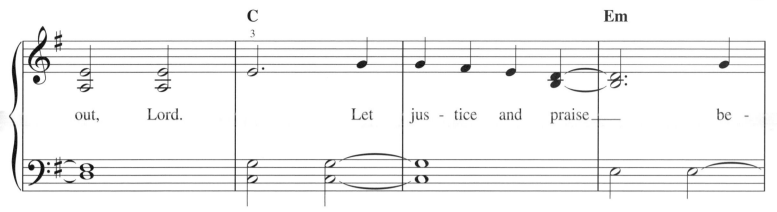

out, Lord.   Let   jus - tice   and   praise_____   be -

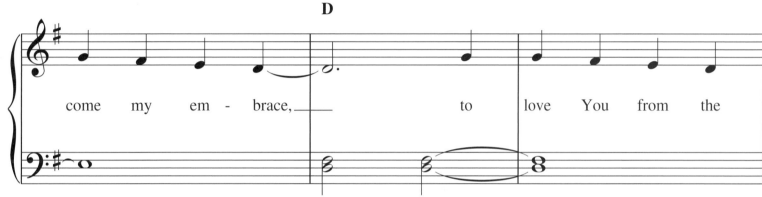

come   my   em - brace,_____   to   love   You   from   the

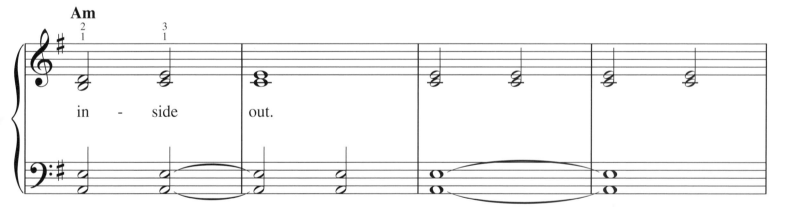

in - side   out.

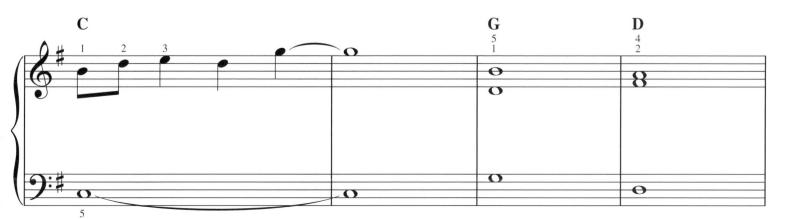

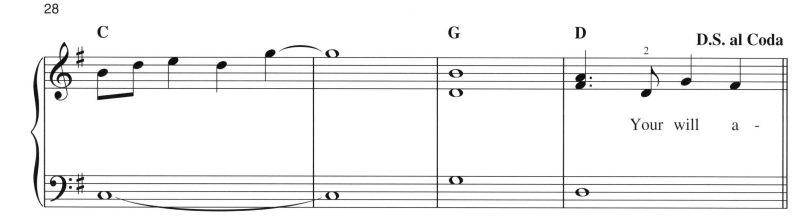

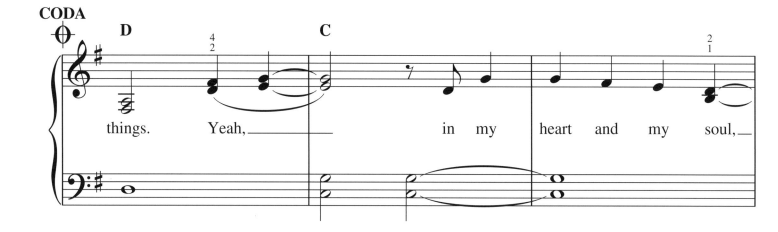

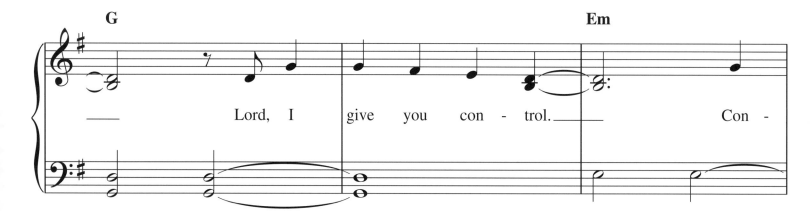

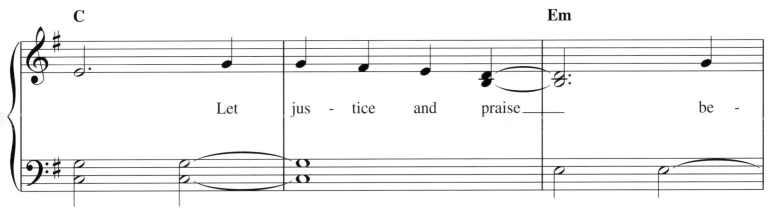

Let jus - tice and praise _____ be -

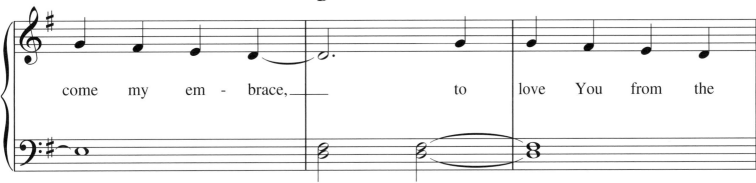

come my em - brace, _____ to love You from the

in - side out. Ev - er - last - ing, Your

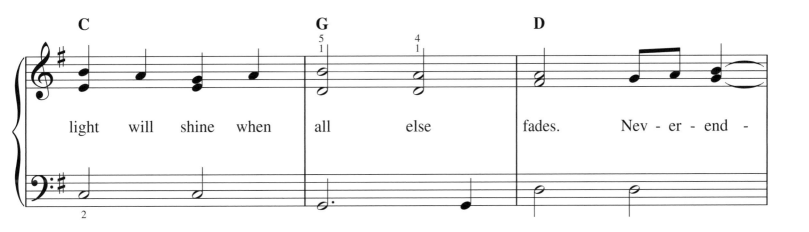

light will shine when all else fades. Nev - er - end -

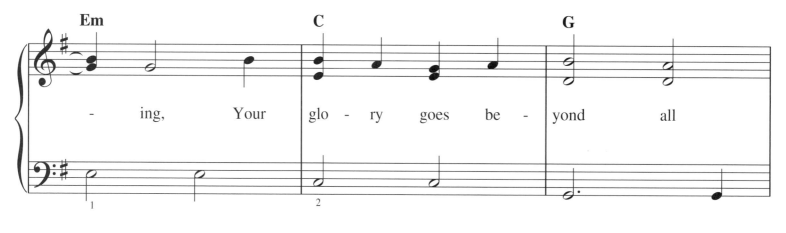

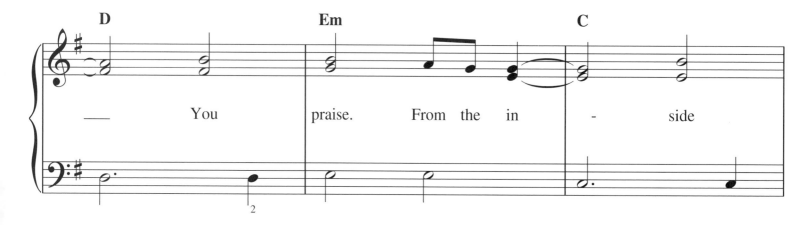

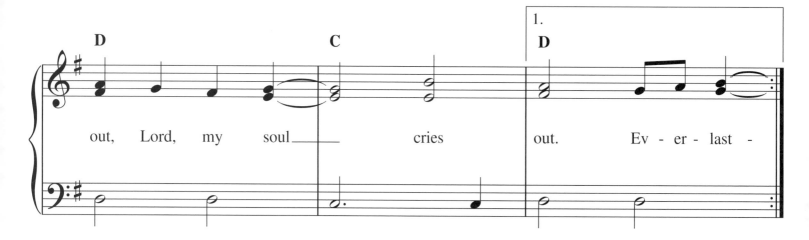

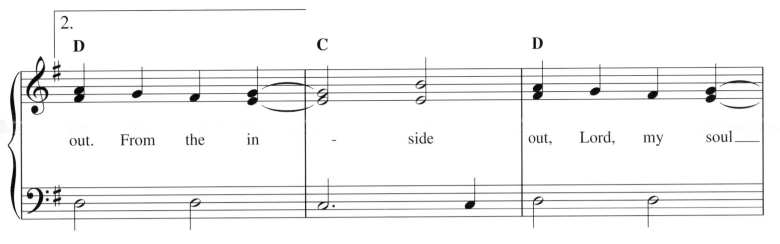

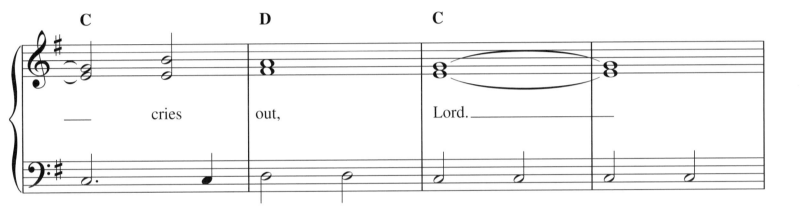

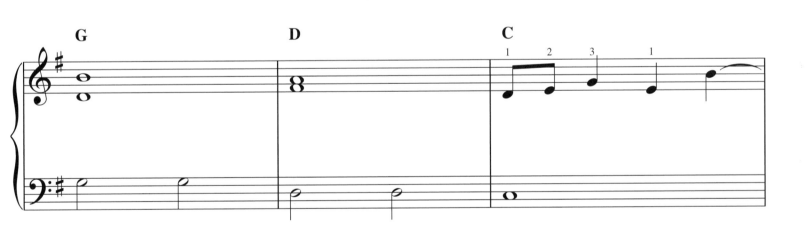

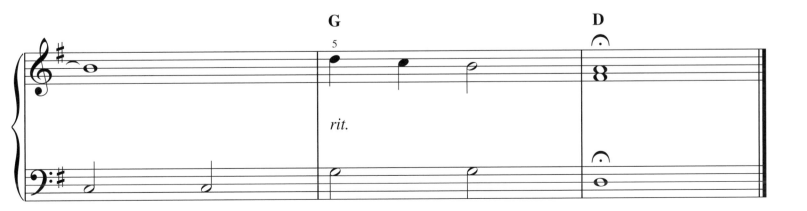

HOLY IS THE LORD

Words and Music by CHRIS TOMLIN
and LOUIE GIGLIO

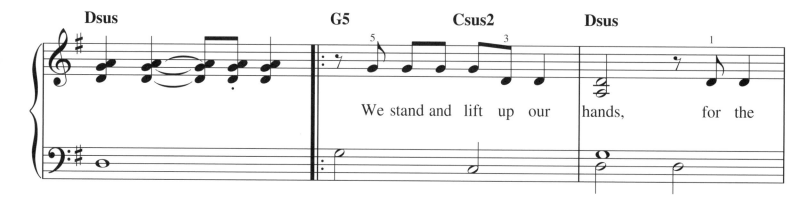

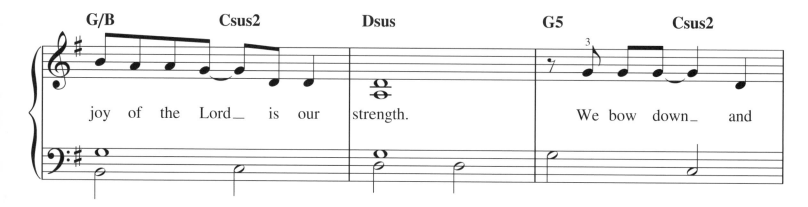

33

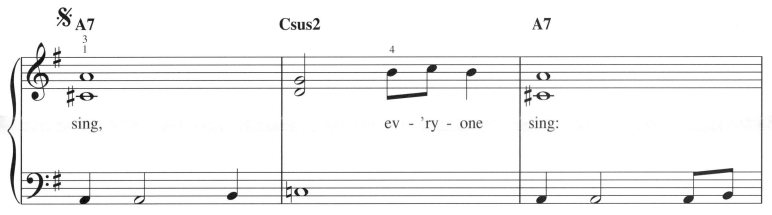

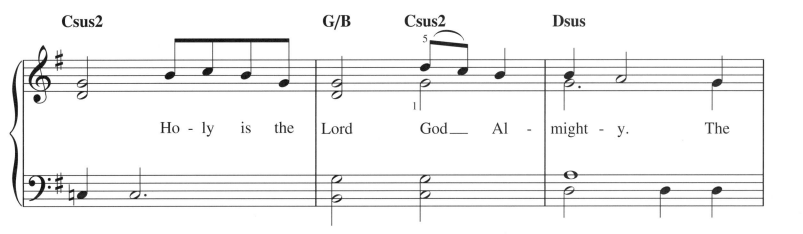

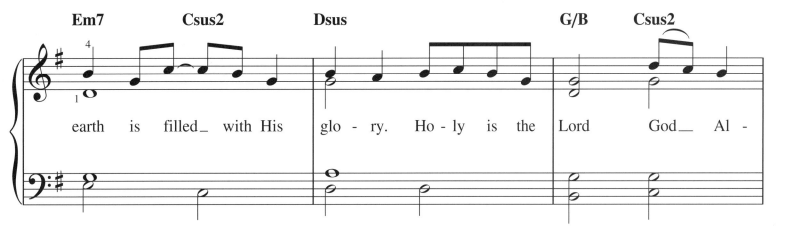

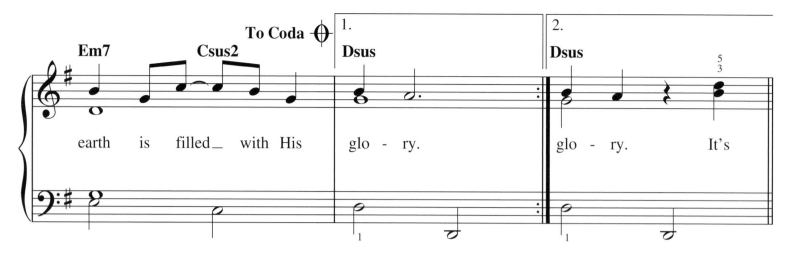

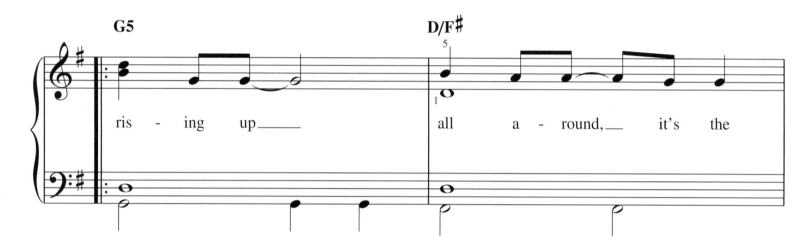

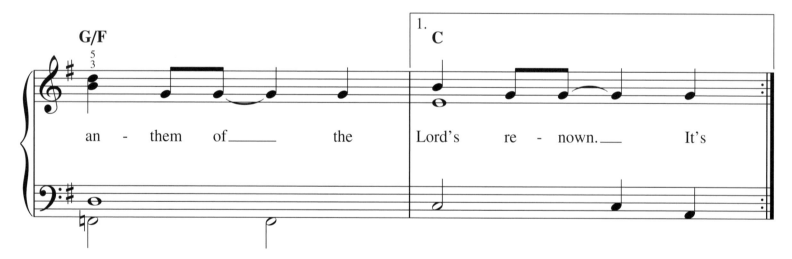

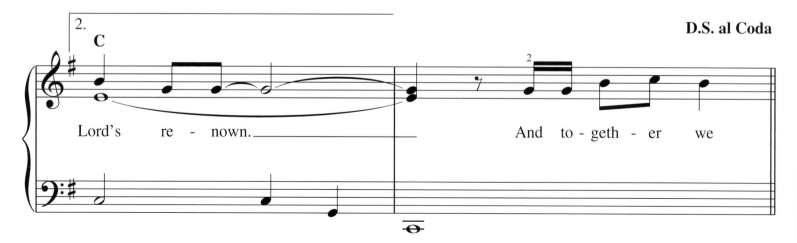

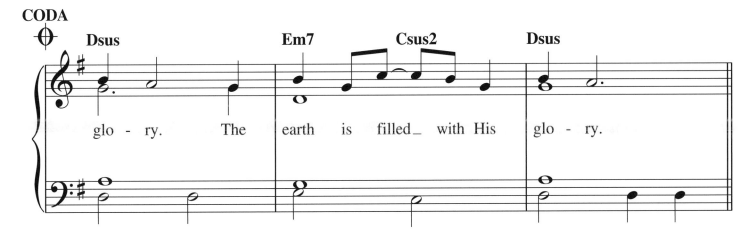

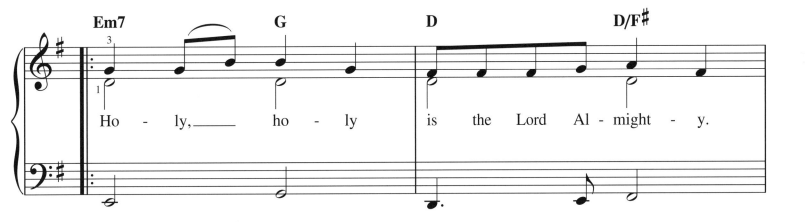

MADE TO WORSHIP

Words and Music by CHRIS TOMLIN,
ED CASH and STEPHAN SHARP

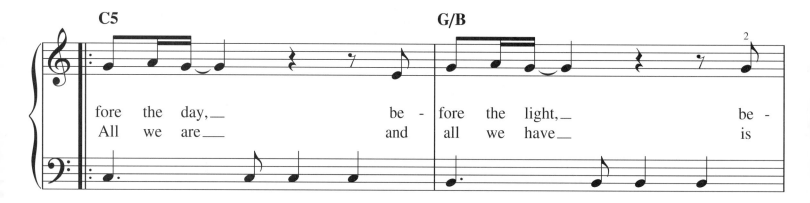

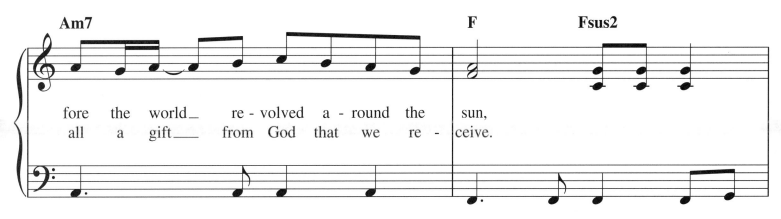

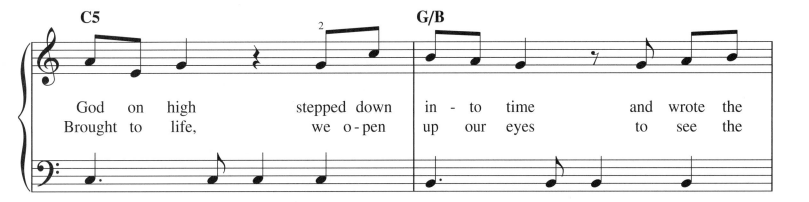

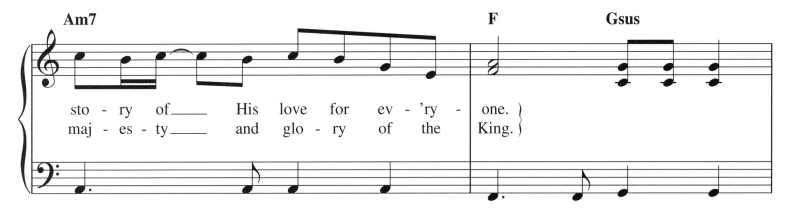

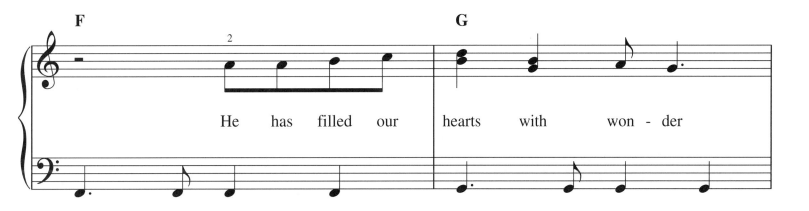

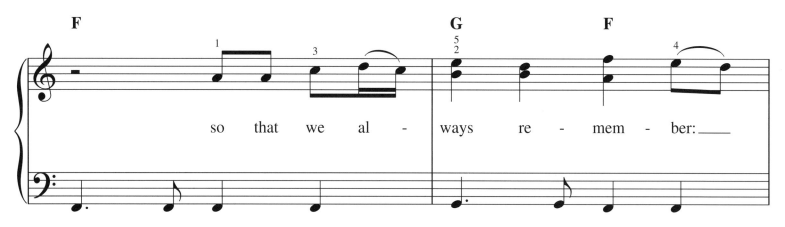

so that we al - ways re - mem - ber:____

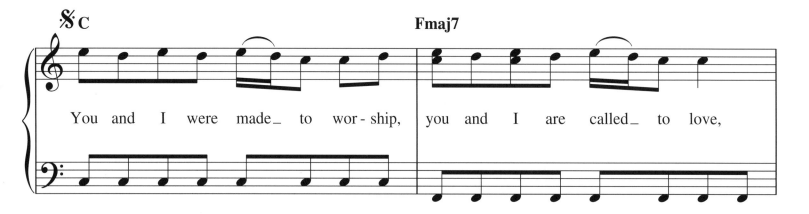

You and I were made_ to wor - ship, you and I are called_ to love,

you and I are for - giv - en and free.____ When

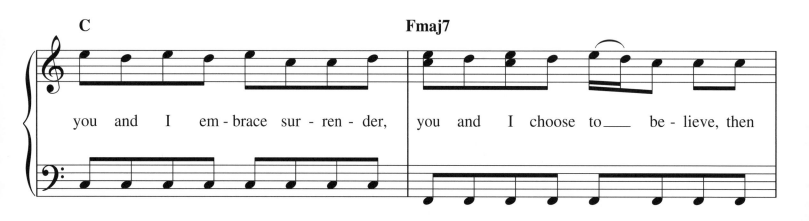

you and I em - brace sur - ren - der, you and I choose to__ be - lieve, then

Dm7   G   To Coda

you   and   I   will   see   who   we   were   meant   to

1.
C5

be.

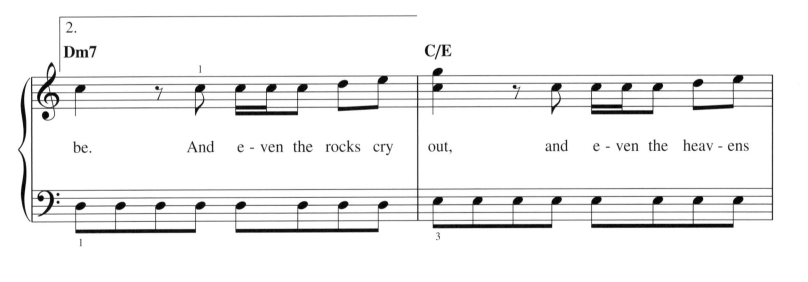

2.
Dm7   C/E

be.   And   e - ven   the   rocks   cry   out,   and   e - ven   the   heav - ens

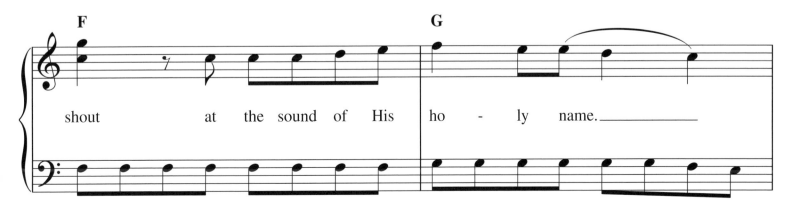

F   G

shout   at   the   sound   of   His   ho - ly   name._____

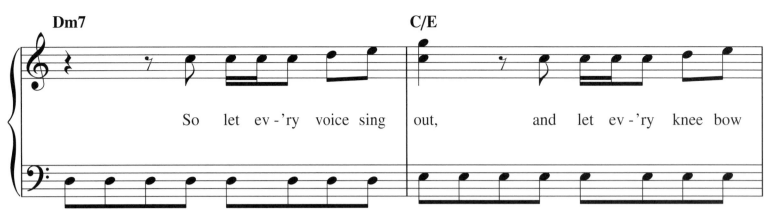

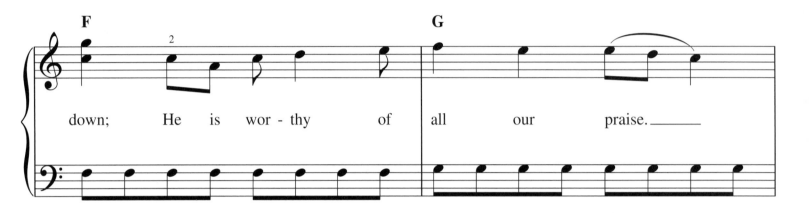

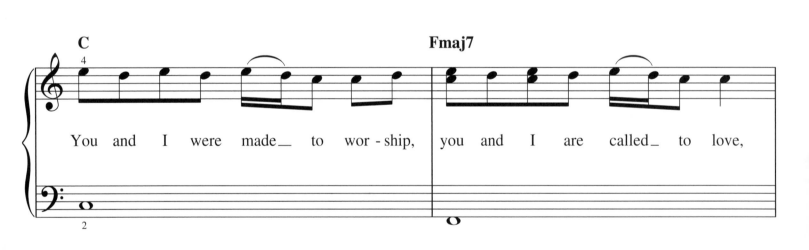

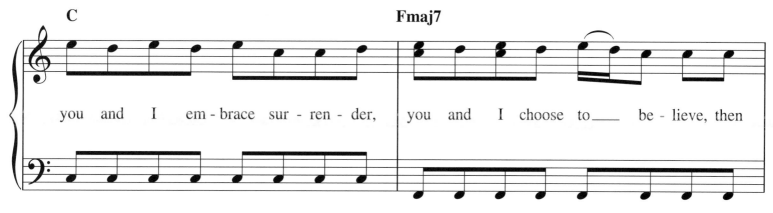

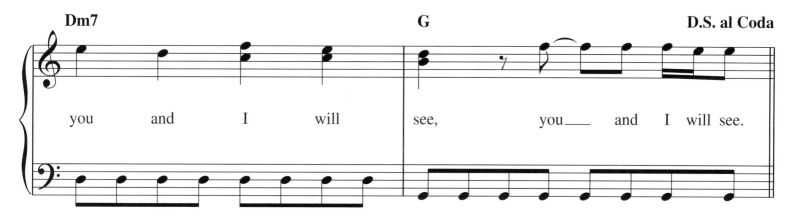

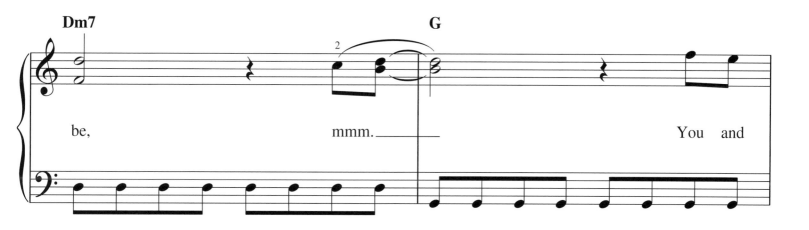

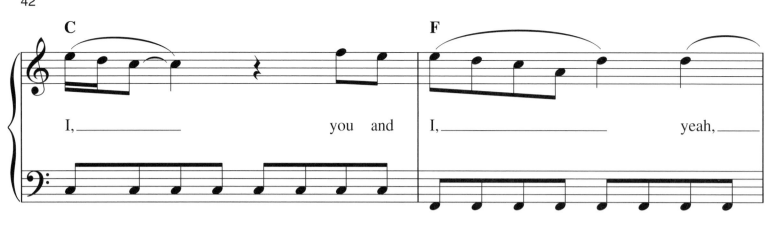

I, _____ you and

I, _____ yeah, ___

___ yeah, _____ mmm, _____ and we were meant to

be.

WHOLLY YOURS

Words and Music by
DAVID CROWDER

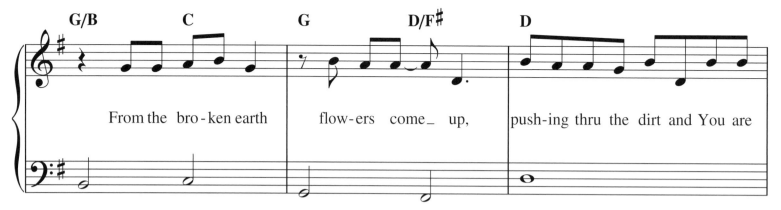

From the bro-ken earth   flow-ers come_ up,   push-ing thru the dirt and You are

ho - ly,   ho - ly,   ho - ly.   All heav-en cries,   "Ho - ly,   ho - ly___

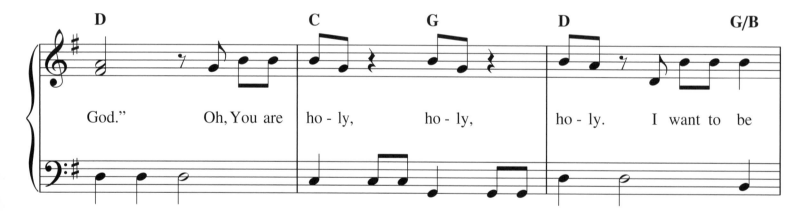

God."   Oh, You are   ho - ly,   ho - ly,   ho - ly.   I want to be

ho - ly   like You_   are._____

45

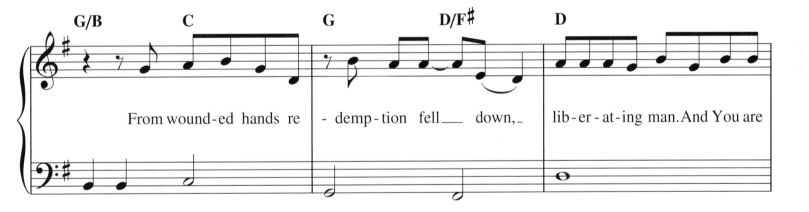

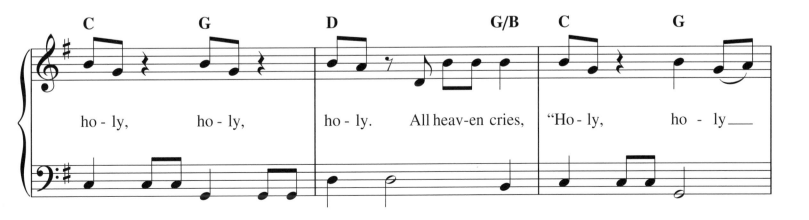

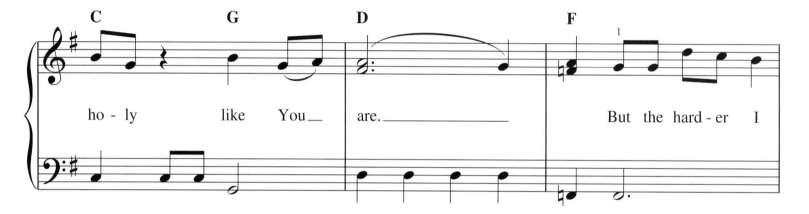

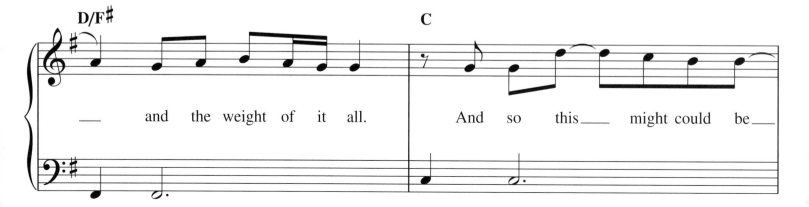

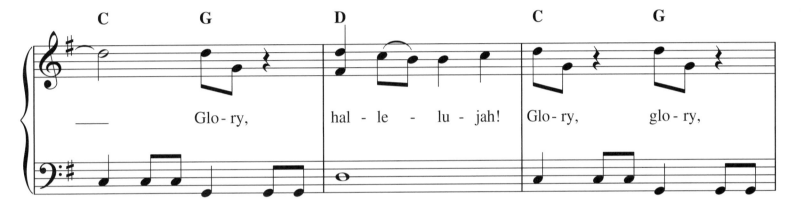

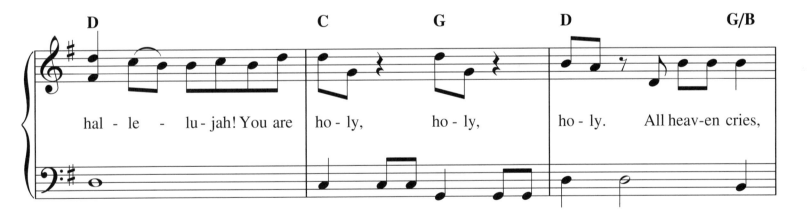

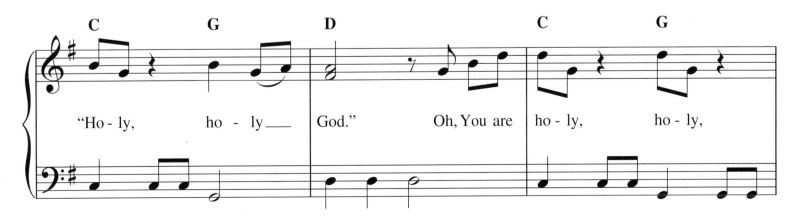

ho - ly. I want to be ho - ly, ho - ly, God. So

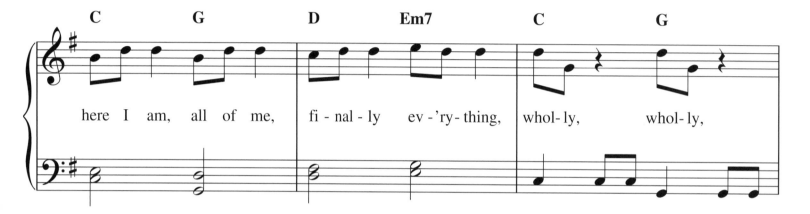

here I am, all of me, fi - nal - ly ev -'ry- thing, whol- ly, whol- ly,

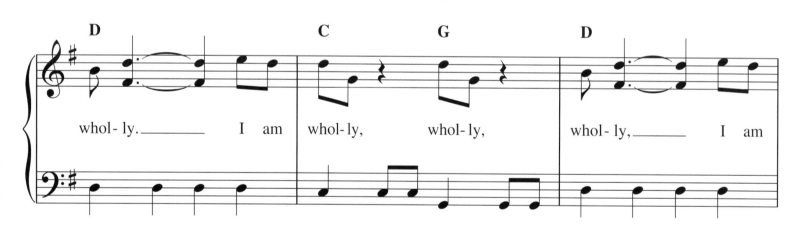

whol- ly._____ I am whol- ly, whol- ly, whol- ly,_____ I am

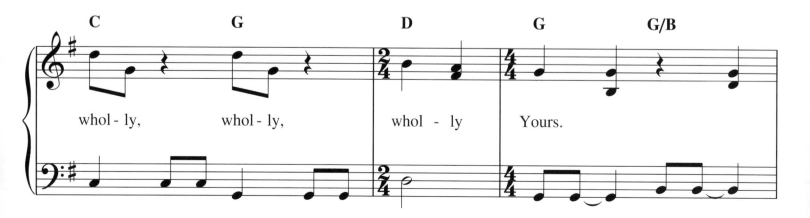

whol - ly, whol - ly, whol - ly Yours.

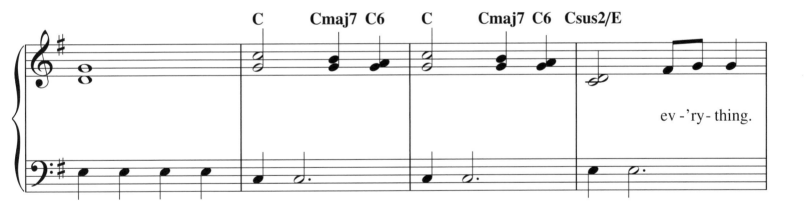

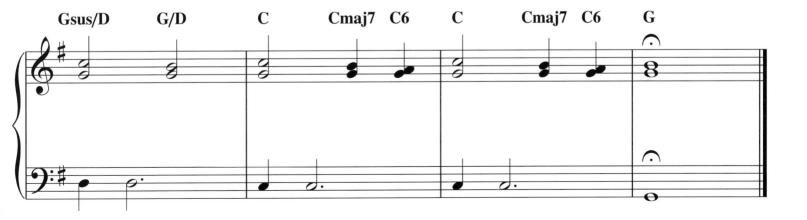

MOUNTAIN OF GOD

Words and Music by MAC POWELL
and BROWN BANNISTER

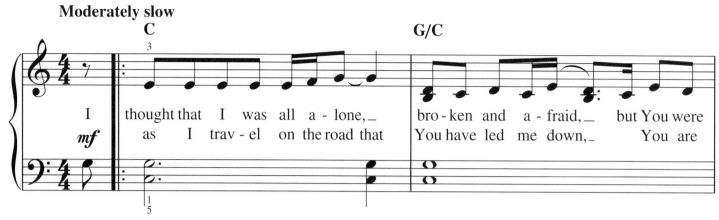

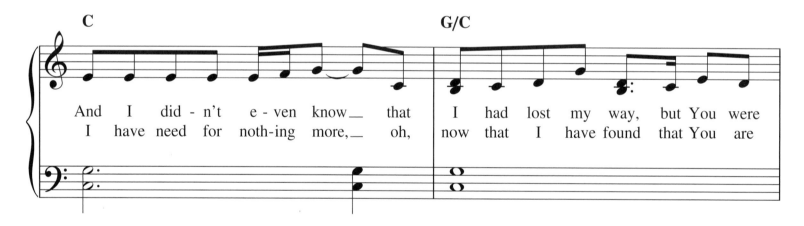

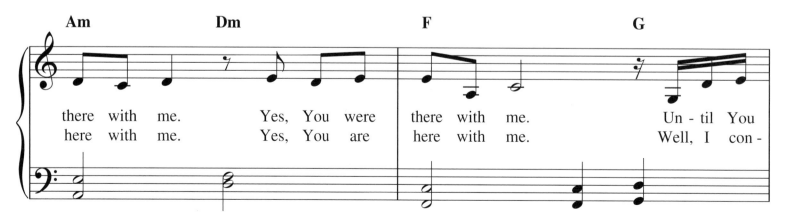

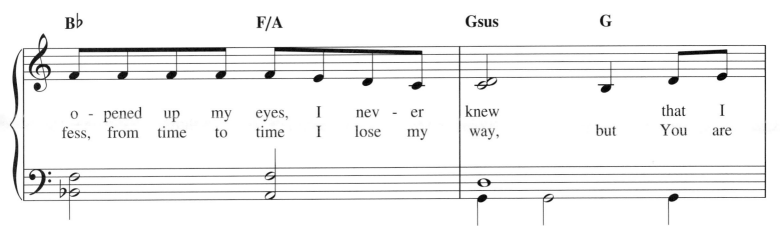

o - pened up my eyes, I nev - er knew that I
fess, from time to time I lose my way, but You are

could - n't ev - er make it with - out You.) And e - ven though the
al - ways there to bring me back a - gain.)

jour - ney's___ long,___ and I know the road is hard, well, the

One who's gone be - fore___ me, He will help me car - ry on. And af - ter all that

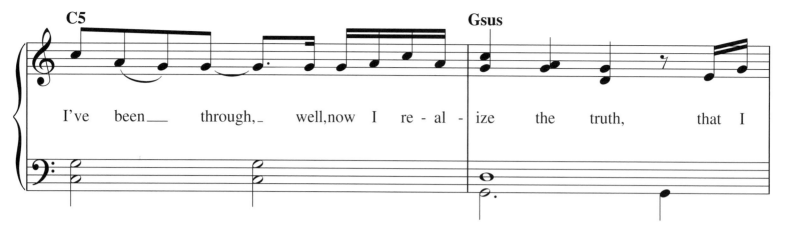

I've been___ through,_ well, now I re-al-ize the truth, that I

must go through the val-ley___ to stand up-on the moun-tain of God._

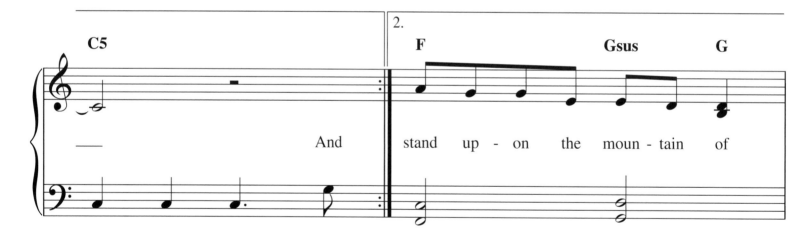

___ And stand up-on the moun-tain of

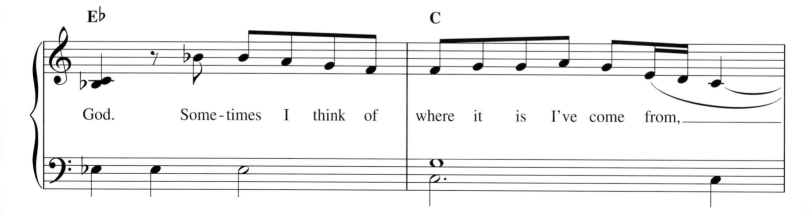

God. Some-times I think of where it is I've come from,___

and the things I've left be - hind._____ But of

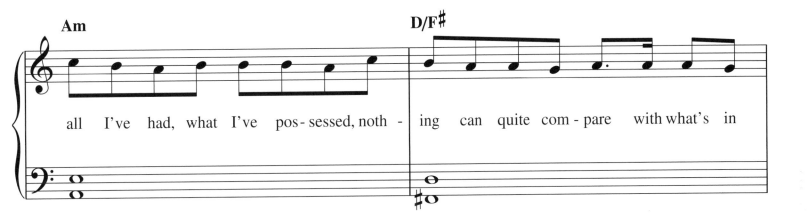

all I've had, what I've pos - sessed, noth - ing can quite com - pare with what's in

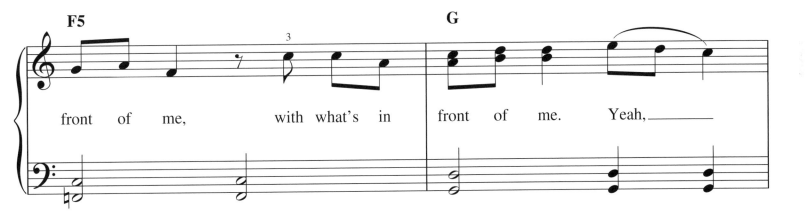

front of me, with what's in front of me. Yeah,_____

yeah._____ E - ven though the jour - ney's long,__ and I know the

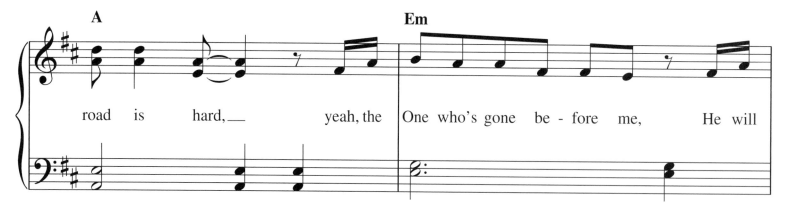

road is hard, ___ yeah, the One who's gone be - fore me, He will

help me car - ry on. And af - ter all that I've been through, ___ now I re - al -

ize the truth, ___ that I must go through the val - ley _____ to

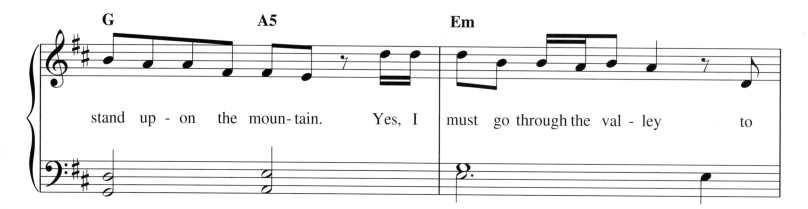

stand up - on the moun - tain. Yes, I must go through the val - ley to

stand up - on the moun-tain. Yes, I must go through the val - ley to

stand up - on the moun - tain.___ I

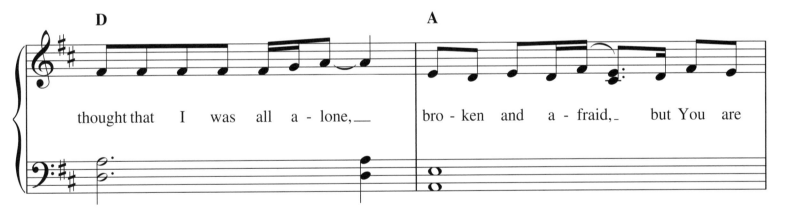

thought that I was all a - lone,___ bro - ken and a - fraid,_ but You are

here with me. Yes, You are here with me.

THE WONDERFUL CROSS

Words and Music by JESSE REEVES,
CHRIS TOMLIN and J.D. WALT

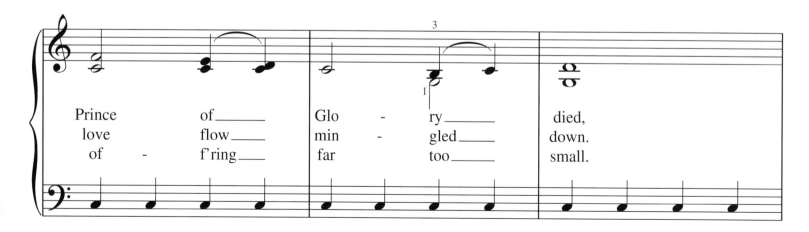

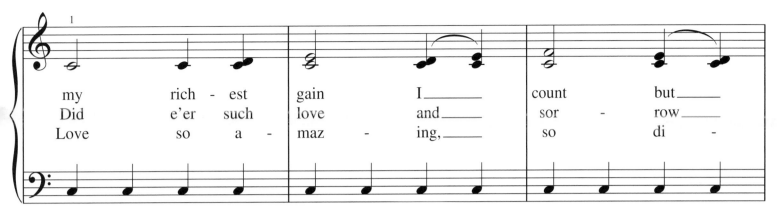

my rich - est gain I_____ count but_____
Did e'er such love and_____ sor - row_____
Love so a - maz - ing,_____ so di -

loss, and pour con - tempt on
meet, or thorns com - pose so
vine, de - mands my soul, so my

1.

all my_____ pride.
rich a_____
life, my_____

2., 3.

crown? }
all. }
O the_____ won - der - ful_____ cross,_____ O the_____

F   C/E

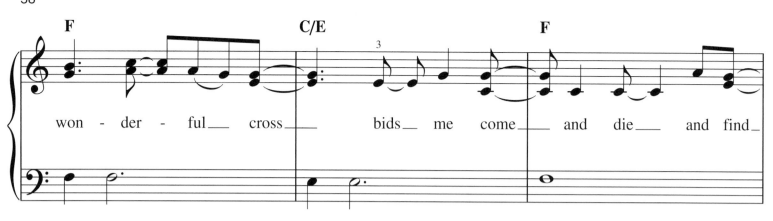

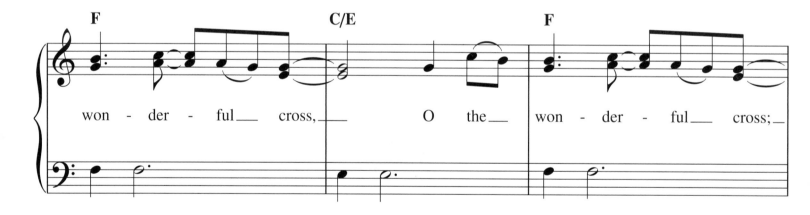

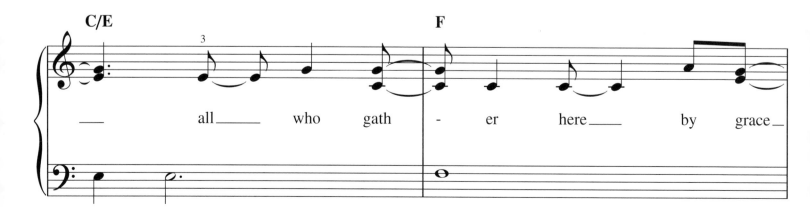

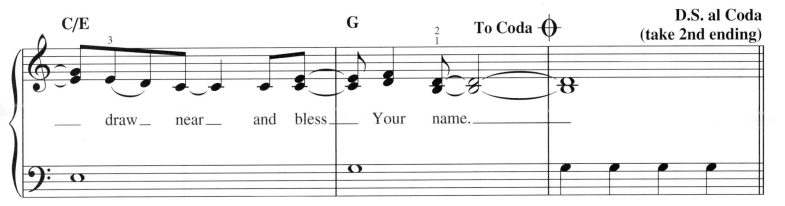

draw___ near___ and bless___ Your name._____

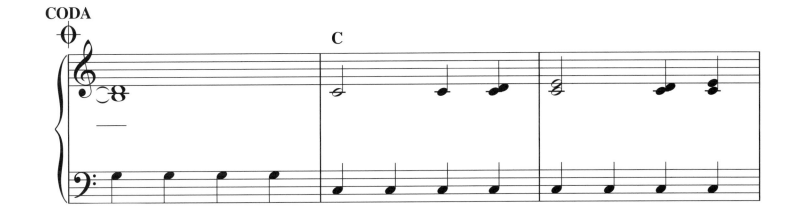

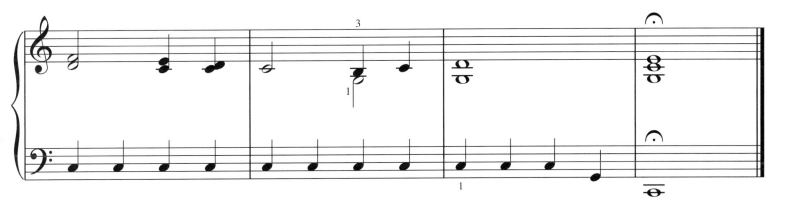

YES YOU HAVE

Words and Music by MATTHEW BRONLEEWE,
LEELAND MOORING and JACK MOORING

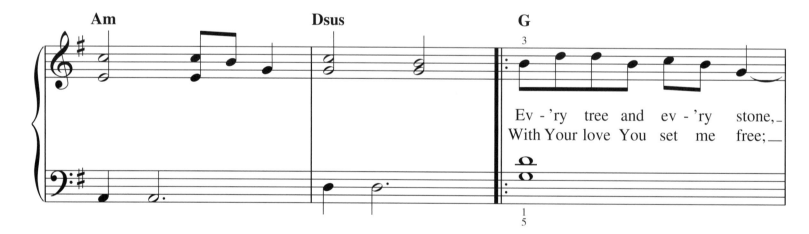

Ev - 'ry tree and ev - 'ry stone,
With Your love You set me free;

ev - 'ry rush-ing wind that moans,   they
three nails gave me lib-er-ty.   So I'll

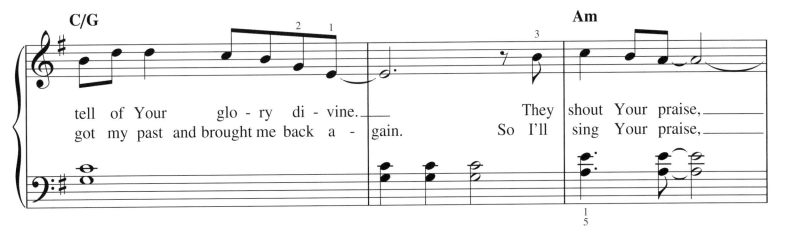

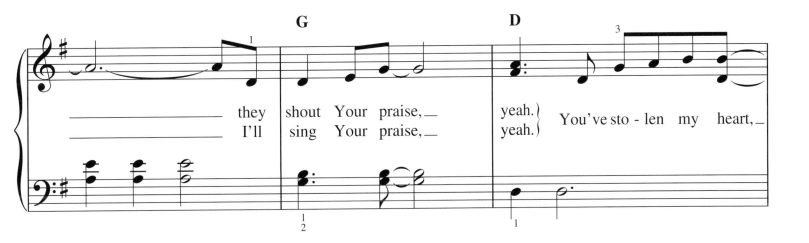

yes, You have. ___ You've sto-len my heart, ___ yes, You have. ___

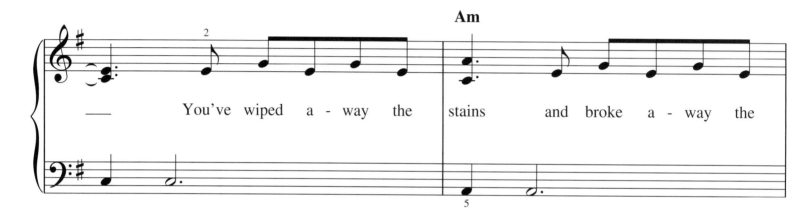

___ You've wiped a - way the stains and broke a - way the

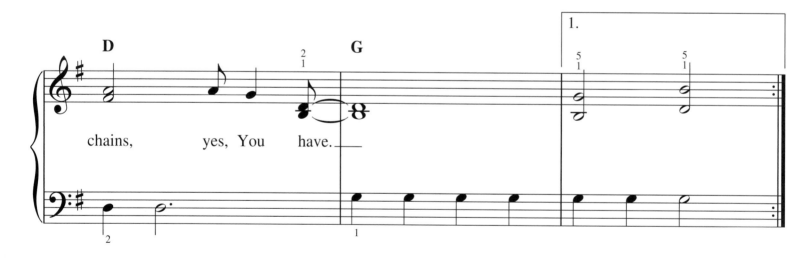

chains, yes, You have. ___

1.

2.

If I as-cend in - to the sky or hide be-hind the

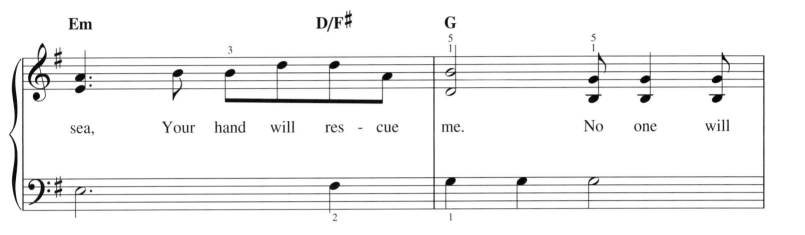

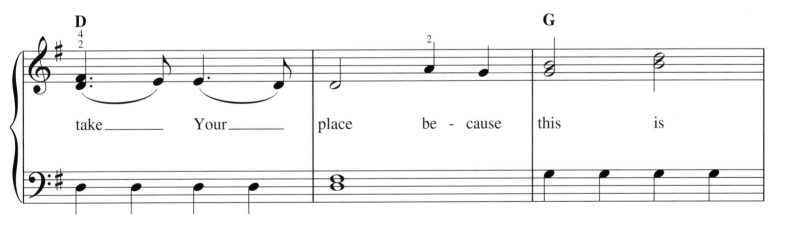

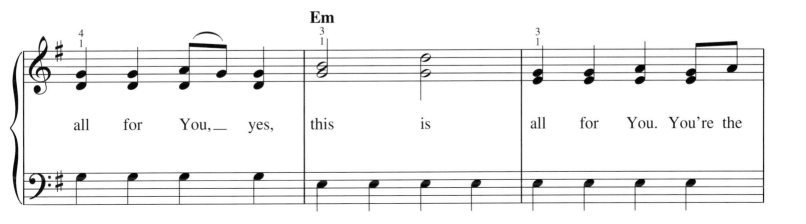

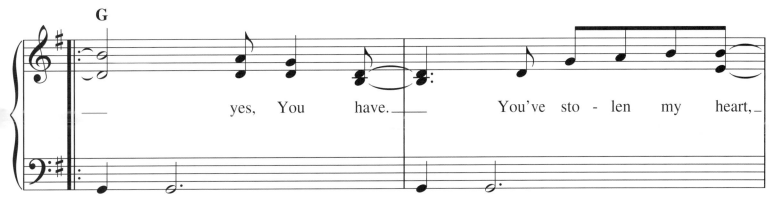

yes, You have. You've sto - len my heart,

yes, You have. You've wiped a - way the

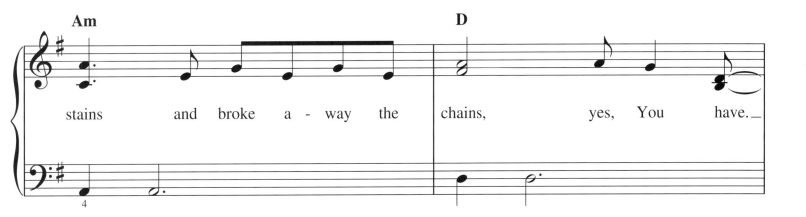

stains and broke a - way the chains, yes, You have.

I know, You've sto - len my heart,

YOU NEVER LET GO

Words and Music by MATT REDMAN
and BETH REDMAN

Joyfully, in 2

E - ven tho' I

walk / light through the / that is val - ley / com - ing of the / for the shad - ow / heart that of / holds death, / on,

Your / a per - fect / glo - rious love / light is / be - cast - ing / yond out / all fear. / com - pare.

And / And e - ven / there will when / be I'm / an caught / end in the / to these

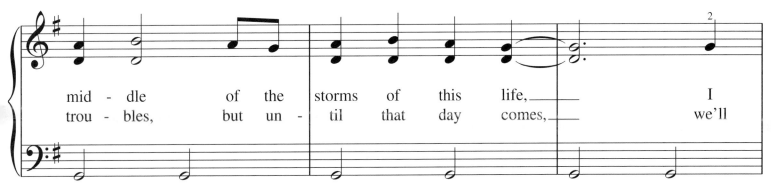

mid - dle of the storms of this life,____ I
trou - bles, but un - til that day comes,____ we'll

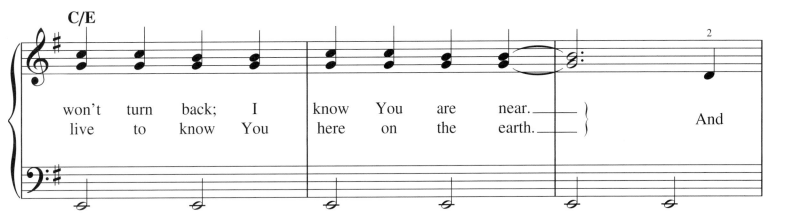

C/E

won't turn back; I know You are near.____ } And
live to know You here on the earth.____

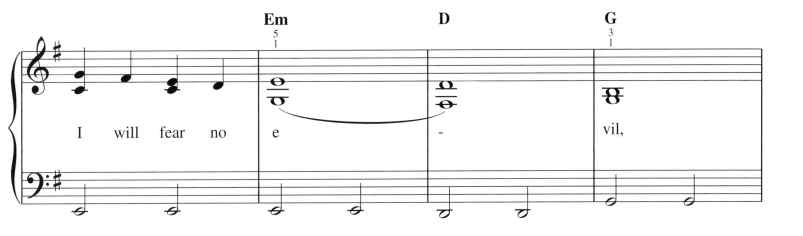

Em   **D**   **G**

I will fear no e - vil,

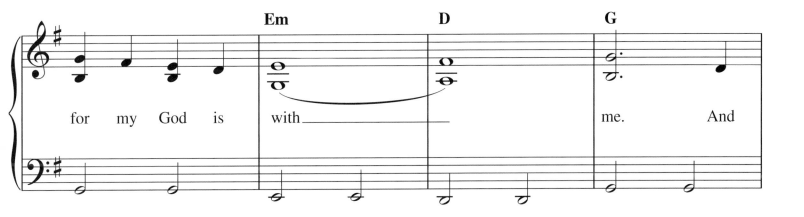

Em   **D**   **G**

for my God is with_____ me. And

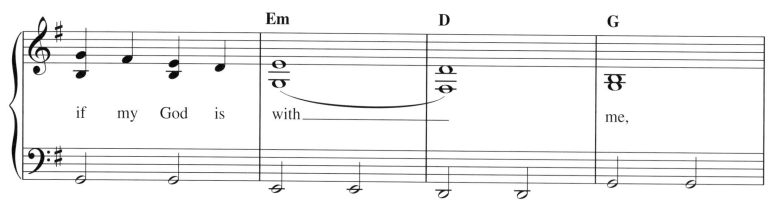

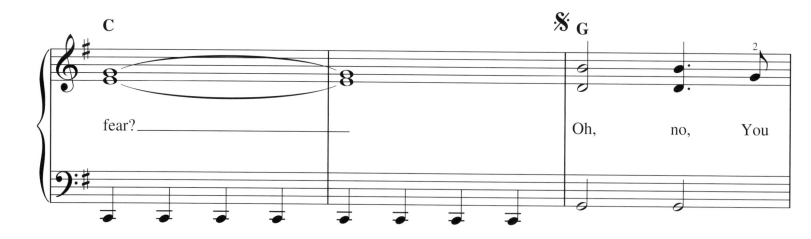

Oh,   no,   You nev-er let go,   in ev-'ry high and

ev - 'ry low.   Oh,   no,   You nev-er let go,

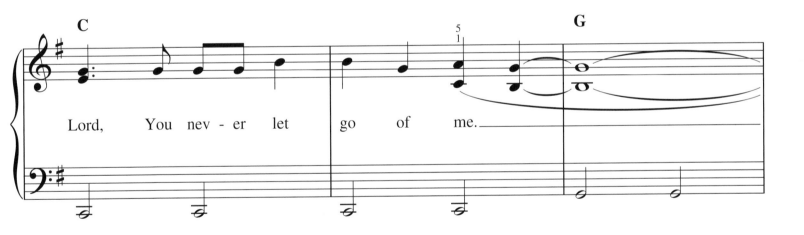

Lord,   You nev-er let   go   of   me.

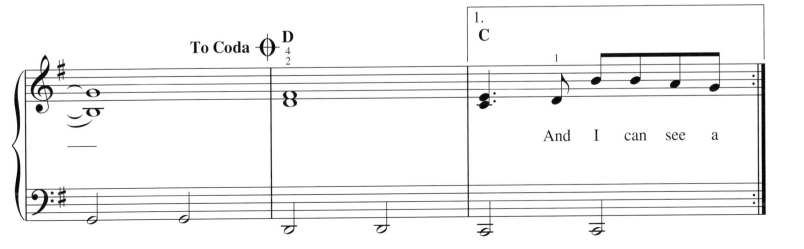

And I can see a

70

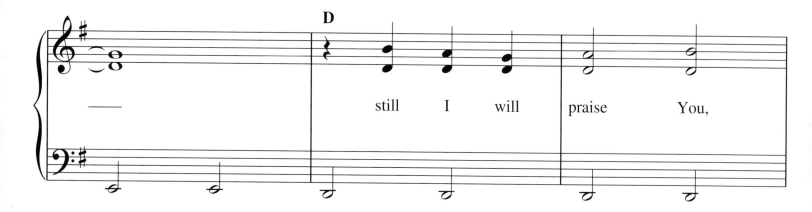

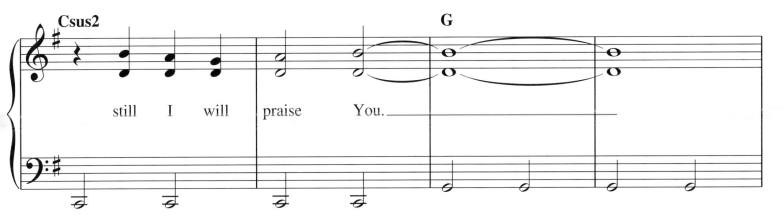

still   I will   praise   You._____

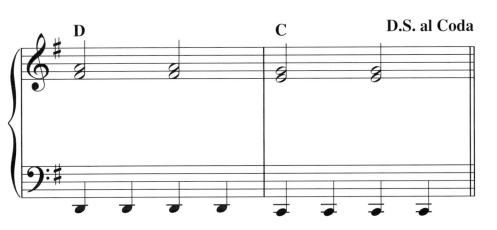

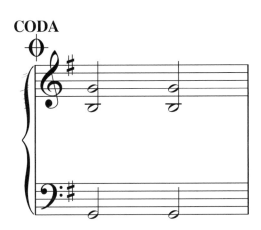

Oh,   no,   You nev - er let   go,

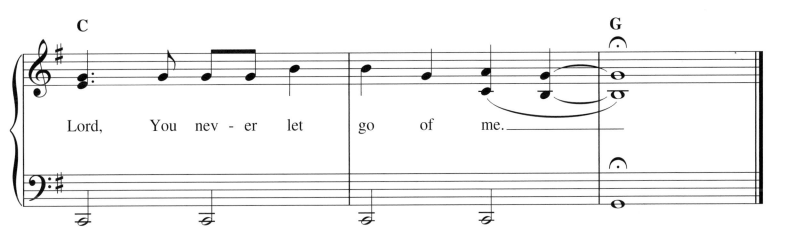

Lord,   You nev - er let go of me._____

The Best Praise & Worship
Songbooks for Piano

Above All
THE PHILLIP KEVEREN SERIES

15 beautiful praise song piano solo arrangements, perfect for home or congregational use. Includes: Agnus Dei • Ancient of Days • Breathe • Draw Me Close • I Stand in Awe • I Want to Know You • More Love, More Power • Step by Step • We Fall Down • more.
00311024 Piano Solo.............................$11.95

The Best of Worship Together®
15 super-popular worship songs: Forever • He Reigns • Here I Am to Worship • Let Everything That Has Breath • and more.
00306635 P/V/G......................................$9.95
00311143 Easy Piano $9.95

The Best Praise & Worship Songs Ever
80 all-time favorites: Breathe • Days of Elijah • Here I Am to Worship • I Could Sing of Your Love Forever • Open the Eyes of My Heart • Shout to the Lord • We Bow Down • dozens more.
00311057 P/V/G....................................$19.95

The Best Praise & Worship Songs Ever – Easy Piano
Over 70 of the best P&W songs today, including: Awesome God • Blessed Be Your Name • Days of Elijah • Here I Am to Worship • Open the Eyes of My Heart • Shout to the Lord • We Fall Down • and more.
00311312 Easy Piano $17.95

Here I Am to Worship
30 top songs from such CCM stars as Rebecca St. James, Matt Redman, and others. Includes: Be Glorified • Enough • It Is You • Let My Words Be Few • Majesty • We Fall Down • You Alone • more.
00313270 P/V/G....................................$14.95

Here I Am to Worship – For Kids
This great songbook lets the kids join in on 20 of the best modern worship songs, including: God of Wonders • He Is Exalted • The Heart of Worship • Song of Love • Wonderful Maker • and more.
00316098 Easy Piano $14.95

I Could Sing of Your Love Forever
THE PHILLIP KEVEREN SERIES

15 worship songs arranged for solo piano: Holy Ground • I Could Sing of Your Love Forever • I Love You Lord • In This Very Room • My Utmost for His Highest • The Potter's Hand • The Power of Your Love • Shout to the North • more.
00310905 Piano Solo.............................$12.95

Modern Worship
THE CHRISTIAN MUSICIAN SERIES

35 favorites of contemporary congregations, including: All Things Are Possible • Ancient of Days • The Heart of Worship • Holiness • I Could Sing of Your Love Forever • I Will Exalt Your Name • It Is You • We Fall Down • You Are My King (Amazing Love) • and more.
00310957 P/V/G....................................$14.95

Shout to the Lord!
THE PHILLIP KEVEREN SERIES

Moving arrangements of 14 praise song favorites, including: As the Deer • Great Is the Lord • More Precious than Silver • Oh Lord, You're Beautiful • Shine, Jesus, Shine • Shout to the Lord • Thy Word • and more.
00310699 Piano Solo.............................$12.95

Timeless Praise
THE PHILLIP KEVEREN SERIES

20 songs of worship arranged for easy piano by Phillip Keveren: El Shaddai • Give Thanks • How Beautiful • How Majestic Is Your Name • Oh Lord, You're Beautiful • People Need the Lord • Seek Ye First • There Is a Redeemer • Thy Word • and more.
00310712 Easy Piano $12.95

Worship Together® Favorites
All Over the World • Cry Out to Jesus • Empty Me • Everlasting God • Forever • Happy Day • Holy Is the Lord • How Deep the Father's Love for Us • How Great Is Our God • Indescribable • Join the Song • Ready for You • Wholly Yours • Yes You Have • You Never Let Go.
00313360 P/V/G....................................$16.95

Worship Together® Favorites for Kids
Enough • Everlasting God • Forever • From the Inside Out • Holy Is the Lord • How Great Is Our God • Made to Worship • Mountain of God • Wholly Yours • The Wonderful Cross • Yes You Have • You Never Let Go.
00316109 Easy Piano $12.95

Worship Together® Platinum
22 of the best contemporary praise & worship songs: Be Glorified • Better Is One Day • Draw Me Close • Every Move I Make • Here I Am to Worship • I Could Sing of Your Love Forever • O Praise Him (All This for a King) • and more.
00306721 P/V/G....................................$16.95

Worship – The Ultimate Collection
Matching folio with 24 top worship favorites, including: God of Wonders • He Reigns • Hungry (Falling on My Knees) • Lord, Reign in Me • Open the Eyes of My Heart • Yesterday, Today and Forever • and more.
00313337 P/V/G....................................$17.95

FOR MORE INFORMATION, SEE YOUR LOCAL MUSIC DEALER,
OR WRITE TO:

HAL•LEONARD® CORPORATION
7777 W. BLUEMOUND RD. P.O. BOX 13819 MILWAUKEE, WI 53213

For complete song lists and to view our entire catalog of titles, please visit www.halleonard.com

Prices, contents, and availability subject to change without notice.

0407